Still
Life

The interior is not a stronghold to be taken by storm and violence, but a kingdom of peace to be gained only by love.
—Jeanne Marie Bouvier de la Mothe.
Madame Guyon

December 1994

To Dearly Beloved JENNI
With all our love in JESUS
this time of His Birthday & may
you find this "Book of Days"
hapful through this 1995
New Year of "Learning to LIVE AGAIN"
with JESUS & His People —
from
Nicholas and Marigold
⊗   ⊗

Jenni Black

Birthday
book!

Still Life

A Book of Days

A LION BOOK
Oxford · Batavia · Sydney

Published by
Lion Publishing Corporation
1705 Hubbard Avenue, Batavia, Illinois 60510, USA
ISBN 0 7459 1808 5
Lion Publishing plc
Sandy Lane West, Littlemore, Oxford, England
ISBN 0 7459 1808 5
Albatross Books Pty Ltd
PO Box 320, Sutherland, NSW 2232, Australia
ISBN 0 7324 0149 6

First edition 1989

Bible quotations are from the Revised Standard Version

Designed by Donna Nelson
Printed in Italy

A Book for Remembering...

birthdays and anniversaries

insights and reflections

plans and events

special days and quiet moments

*A moment's insight
is sometimes worth a
life's experience.*
—Oliver Wendell Holmes

January

All our care should be directed toward acquiring the greatest degree of inward recollection. Nor should we be discouraged by the difficulties we encounter in this exercise, which will soon be recompensed on the part of God. Abundant supplies of grace will render it perfectly easy, provided we are faithful in withdrawing our hearts from outward distractions and occupations, and returning to our center with affections full of tenderness and serenity.
—Jeanne Marie Bouvier de la Mothe. Madame Guyon

January

1

Silence is the element in which great things fashion themselves together, that at length they may emerge, full-formed and majestic, into the daylight of life, which they are henceforth to rule.
—Maurice Maeterlinck

2

3

4

Amabel·Kerr
1995

5

6

7

January

8

9

When you pray, gather up your whole self, enter with your Beloved into the chamber of your heart, and there remain alone with him, forgetting all exterior concerns. And so rise aloft with all your love and all your mind, your affections, your desires and devotion. And let not your mind wander away from your prayer, but rise again and again in the fervor of your piety until you enter into the place of the wonderful tabernacle, even the house of God. There your heart will be delighted at the sight of your Beloved, and you will taste and see how good the Lord is and how great is his goodness.
—St. Bonaventure

10

11

12

January

13

14

15

16

17

Charlotte

18

The steadfast love of the Lord never ceases,
his mercies never come to an end;
they are new every morning;
great is thy faithfulness.
The Lord is good to those who wait for him,
to the soul that seeks him.
It is good that one should wait quietly for the salvation of the Lord.
—Lamentations 3:22-23, 25

January

19

Jemima
,9· 99

20

21

22
_____

23
_____

*S*olitude is a wonderful thing when one is at
peace with oneself and when there is a definite task to
be accomplished.
—Johann Wolfgang von Goethe

24
_____

January

John Napier

25
_____

26
_____

**B**reathe through the heats of our desire
Thy coolness and thy balm.
Let sense be dumb, let flesh retire;
Speak through the earthquake, wind, and fire,
O still small voice of calm!
—John Greenleaf Whittier

27
_____

28

29

30

31

February

*Lord, make me an
instrument of your peace.
Where there is hatred, let
me sow love; where there
is injury, pardon; where
there is doubt, faith;
where there is despair,
hope; where there is
darkness, light; where
there is sadness, joy.
O Divine Master, grant
that I may not so much
seek to be consoled as
to console, not so much
to be understood as to
understand, not so much
to be loved as to love; for
it is in giving that we
receive; it is in pardoning
that we are pardoned; it is
in dying that we awake to
eternal life.*
—Attributed to
St. Francis of Assisi

Like a bird that trails a broken wing, I have come home to thee.
—Ellen Gilbert

February

Sue Napier ?

1

Fergus Black 1994

Lucinda Dashwood

2

3

4

February

5

When the voices of children are heard on the green
And laughing is heard on the hill,
My heart is at rest within my breast
And everything else is still.
—William Blake

6

7

February

8

9

*We cannot kindle when we will
The fire that in the heart resides,
The spirit bloweth and is still,
In mystery our soul abides.*
—Matthew Arnold

10

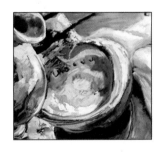

11

12

February

13

Finn Napier 2005
Johnny Boscawen

> *D*o not forget
> *prayer. Every time you*
> *pray, if your prayer is*
> *sincere, there will be new*
> *feeling and new meaning*
> *in it, which will give you*
> *fresh courage.*
> —Fyodor Dostoyevski

14

15

February

16

17

*O*ur life is frittered away by detail...
Simplify, simplify.
—Henry David Thoreau

18

February

We must live in simplicity, with neither pretensions nor mannerisms nor servile fear; we must walk in the light of a living faith that shines in more than mere words; and always so, in adversity as well as in prosperity, in times of persecution as well as in consolation. Nothing will be able to change either the strength or the radiance of our faith if the Truth has given us knowledge of truth, not just in desire but in living experience.
—Catherine of Sienna

19

20 She Napier

21

*B*etter to remain
silent and be thought a
fool than to speak and to
remove all doubt.
—Abraham Lincoln

22

23

February

24

25   *Patricia Wallace*

26

27

*W*hat made the most profound impact on me was the depth of the silence. I ate in the refectory with the sisters—in silence. I prayed in the chapel with the sisters each morning—in silence. Like them, I spent most of my day in silence. The power this silence generated stunned me.
—Joyce Huggett

Nia Black

28

29

March

Jesus told his disciples to cultivate a still center inside themselves. "When you pray, go into your room and shut the door and pray to your Father who is in secret" (Matthew 6:6).... Jesus must... have been speaking not only of a secret place... but of that "portable inner sanctuary" which we carry around with us and to which we can withdraw at any time and in any place....Wherever or whatever, we are free to move back and forth across the threshold of this inner place of solitude and prayer, to commune with God unnoticed and unknown by any other human being.
—Margaret Magdalen

March

1 *Jamie Black*

2

It is easy in the world to live after the world's opinion; it is easy in solitude to live after your own; but the great man is he who in the midst of the crowd keeps with perfect sweetness the independence of solitude.
—Ralph Waldo Emerson

March

Meg Connelley 1995?

3

My soul finds rest in God alone; my salvation comes from him.
—Psalm 62:1

4

(Robin)

James Napier

5

March

6

The very best and utmost attainment in this life is to remain still and let God act and speak in you.
—Meister Eckhart

7

8

9

_____

10

_____

*I*t is not enough
that we pray outwardly
only with the mouth; true
prayer, the best prayer,
takes place in the inner
person, and either breaks
out verbally or remains
hidden in the soul.
—Philip Jacob Spener

11

_____

March

12 _____

13 _____

Gordon Palmer

14 _____

15 _____

In his will is our peace.
—Dante

16

17

18

19

March

20

21

22

Sweet are the thoughts that savor of content;
The quiet mind is richer than a crown.
—Robert Greene

23

24

25

March

26

27
(Daddy)

28

29

30

*M*y whole soul
was filled with the
unutterable peace of the
undisturbed opportunity
for communion with
God—with the sense that
at last I had found a place
where I might, without
the faintest suspicion of
insincerity, join with
others in simply seeking
His presence.
—Caroline Stephen

Minna Kerr
1998

31

April

If a tiny spark of God's love already burns within you, do not expose it to the wind, for it may get blown out. Keep the stove tightly shut so that it will not lose its heat and grow cold. In other words, avoid distraction as well as you can. Stay quiet with God.
—Charles Borromeo

The heart has its reasons that reason can never know.
—Blaise Pascal

April

1

2

3

4

5

Accustom yourself to the wonderful thought that God loves you with a tenderness, a generosity, and an intimacy which surpasses all your dreams. Give yourself up with joy to a loving confidence in God, and have courage to believe firmly that God's action towards you is a masterpiece of partiality and love. Rest tranquilly in this abiding conviction.
—Henri de Tourville

6

April

7 April Rivett-Carnac

8

Have no anxiety
about anything, but in
everything by prayer and
supplication with
thanksgiving let your
requests be made known
to God. And the peace of
God, which passes all
understanding, will keep
your hearts and your
minds in Christ Jesus.
—The Apostle Paul, in
Philippians 4:6-7

April

9

Judy Boscawen

10

Rose Connelley

11

April

12

Peace is a precious treasure to be sought out with great zeal....Live your life that you may receive the blessings of the Lord. Then the peace of God our Father will be with you always.
—Francis Paolo

13

Jess Sykes

14

Marion Martineau

Charlie Napier

15

16

17

April

18 marie claire Kerr

It is difficult to be quiet if you have nothing to do.
—Arthur Schopenhauer

19

20

April

21
_____

22
_____

23
_____

24
_____

April

25 _____

26 _____

27 _____

28

29

---

*I*f we have not quiet
in our minds, outward
comfort will do no more
for us than a golden
slipper on a gouty foot.
—John Bunyan

30

May

Just as a person may enjoy the flavor of the finest foods in chewing them; yet receive no nourishment if he does not stop chewing and swallow; so when our affections are kindled, if we try to keep stirring them up, we extinguish the flame and the soul is deprived of its nourishment. Therefore, we should swallow the blessed food we have received in a repose of love, full of respect and confidence. This will advance the soul more in a short time than some other method will in years.

—Jeanne Marie Bouvier de la Mothe. Madame Guyon

May

1

Peace I leave with you; my peace I give to you; not as the world gives do I give to you. Let not your hearts be troubled, neither let them be afraid.
—Jesus, quoted in John 14:27

2

3

4

5

6

7

May

8

9

There was once in man a true happiness, of which there now remains to him only an empty trace which he vainly tries to fill out of his environment. He seeks from things absent the help he cannot obtain from things present. Yet all these efforts are inadequate, because the infinite abyss can only be filled by an infinite and immutable object, that is, by God himself.
—Blaise Pascal

She Jones

10

For solitude sometimes is best society, And short retirement urges sweet return.
—John Milton

Xandra Annelley 1962

11

12

May

13

14

I never found the companion that was so companionable as solitude.
—Henry David Thoreau

15

16

17

18

Jane Ffennell

19

May

20

21

I love tranquil solitude
And such society
As is quiet, wise, and good.
—Percy Bysshe Shelley

22

Ros Gay

23

24

May

25

26

27

28

29

If we are to witness to Christ in today's market places, where there are constant demands on our whole person, we need silence. If we are to be always available, not only physically, but by empathy, sympathy, friendship, understanding. . . , we need silence. To be able to give joyous, unflagging hospitality, not only of house and food, but of mind, heart, body and soul, we need silence.
—Catherine de Hueck Doherty

30

31

June

Keep an open mind, and listen to the still small voice of God that I am sure speaks to thy inner self. To His loving care I commit thee, and, even though thee may not yet thyself know Him, He will always surround thee with His love.
—Hannah Whitall Smith

What peace can they have who are not at peace with God?
—Matthew Henry

June

1 _____

2 _____

3 *Leila Daw.* _____

Lord, grant us calm, if calm can set forth thee.
—Christina Rossetti

4

5

I value society for the abundance of ideas that it
brings before us, . . . but I value solitude for sincerity
and peace, and for the better understanding of the
thoughts that are truly ours.
—Philip Gilbert Hamerton

6

June

7

Claudia Black 1996

8

_I_t is vain that you
rise up early and go late
to rest, eating the bread of
anxious toil; for [the Lord]
gives to his beloved sleep.
—Psalm 127:2

9

10

Tess Liddiard

11

June

12

Zoë Palmer

13

14

15

16

*N*ot *every truth is the better for showing its*
face undisguised; and often silence is the wisest thing
to heed.
—Pindar

17

June

18 _____ mongold Rivett-Carnac _____

19 _____

*A*n elegant
sufficiency, content,
Retirement, rural quiet,
friendship, books.
—James Thompson

20 _____

June

21

22

23

Ann Conan. 1940

24

June

25

No one would talk much in society, if he knew how often he misunderstands others.
—Johann Wolfgang von Goethe

Alastair Palmer
1984

26

27

June

28

29

You have made us for yourself, O Lord, and
our hearts are restless until they rest in you.
—St. Augustine

30

July

When will you ever, Peace, wild wooddove, shy wings shut,
Your round me roaming end, and under be my boughs?
When, when, Peace, will you, Peace? I'll not play hypocrite
To own my heart; I yield you do come sometimes; but
That piecemeal peace is poor peace. What pure peace allows
Alarms of wars, the daunting wars, the death of it?

O surely, reaving Peace, my Lord should leave in lieu
Some good! And so he does leave Patience exquisite,
That plumes to Peace thereafter. And when Peace here does house
He comes with work to do, he does not come to coo,
He comes to brood and sit.
—Gerard Manley Hopkins

July

A little with quiet
Is the only diet.
—George Herbert

1

2

3

4

5

6

7

8

July

9

10

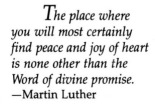

The place where you will most certainly find peace and joy of heart is none other than the Word of divine promise.
—Martin Luther

11

12

13

July

14 _____

15 _____

16 _____

17

18

*E*nter into the inner chamber of your mind. Shut out all things save God and whatever may aid you in seeking God; and having barred the door of your chamber, seek him.
—St. Anselm of Canterbury

19

July

20

_____

21

*T*alking and eloquence are not the same: to speak, and to speak well, are two things. A fool may talk, but a wise man speaks.
—Ben Jonson

22

I have been devotional and my mind has been led away from the follies that it is mostly wrapped up in.
—Elizabeth Fry

Hatching & Cottage

23

24

July

25

26

*The Christian's peace and joy are not
obtained—as are those which the world gives—
through feeling and sensation but through faith.*
—Martin Luther

27

July

28

29

30

31

August

❧

He that is full of peace is suspicious of no one,
but he that is discontented and troubled is tossed with
suspicions. He is not peaceful himself, nor can he
leave others in peace.
—Thomas a Kempis

August

1

2

Lord, I am thine. . . .Work in me all the good pleasures of thy will, and I will only lie still in thy hands and trust thee.
—Hannah Whitall Smith

3

4

Hachiko leave Cottage

5

6

7

August

Johnny Kerr

8

The mind is its own place, and in itself
Can make a heaven of hell, a hell of heaven.
—John Milton

9

10

August

11

12

*A*ll the troubles of
life come upon us because
we refuse to sit quietly for
a while each day in our
rooms.
—Blaise Pascal

13

August

14

Hugh Kerr 1999

15

16

17

18

And so I find it well to come
For deeper rest to this still room;
For here the habit of the soul
Feels less the outer world's control.
And from the silence, multiplied
By these still forms on every side,
The world that time and sense have known
Falls off and leaves us God alone.
—John Greenleaf Whittier

19

20

August

21

22

In this Silence, the mind as well as the tongue *must be stilled. And why?...The mind's tendency to pride, to disputation, to preoccupation with irrelevant abstractions. Moreover, its very busyness tends to keep us conscious of our own efforts, instead of waiting for what may be "given" from the depths.*
—Teresina R. Havens

August

23

24

25

August

26

27

28

August

29

30

*In returning and
rest you shall be saved; in
quietness and in trust
shall be your strength.*
—Isaiah 30:15

31

September

Give me my scallop shell of quiet,
My staff of faith to walk upon,
My scrip of joy, immortal diet,
My bottle of salvation,
My gown of glory, hope's true gage
And thus I'll take my pilgrimage.
—Sir Walter Raleigh

September

1 _____

2 _____

3 _____

4 _____

5

Thou Lord, alone, art all thy children need
And there is none beside;
From thee the streams of blessedness proceed;
In thee the blest abide,
Fountain of life and all-abounding grace,
Our source, our center and our dwelling place!
—Jeanne Marie Bouvier de la Mothe. Madame Guyon

6

7

September

8

9

It is a beauteous evening, calm and free,
The holy time is quiet as a nun
Breathless with adoration.
—William Wordsworth

10

11

12

September

13 _____

14 _____

15 _____
   Amanda Trafford

16

17

A strong, resolute
soul can live in the world
without being infected by
any of its moods, find
sweet springs of piety
amid its salty waves, and
fly through flames of
earthly lusts without
burning the wings of its
holy desires for a devout
life.
—St. Francis of Sales

18

September

19
_____

20
_____

Do not be quick with your mouth, do not be hasty in your heart to utter anything before God. God is in heaven and you are on earth, so let your words be few.
—Ecclesiastes 5:2

September

21

Life being very short, and the quiet hours of it few, we ought to waste none of them in reading valueless books.
—John Ruskin

22

23

September

24

Everyone is always rushing, rushing...I
wonder where they think they're going?
—Mabel Buck, aged 101

25

26

September

Isabella Connelley

27

28

29

30

October

Now stir the fire, and close the shutters fast,
Let fall the curtains, wheel the sofa round,
And, while the bubbling and loud-hissing urn
Throws up a steamy column, and the cups,
That cheer but not inebriate, wait on each,
So let us welcome peaceful evening in.
—William Cowper

October

1
_____

2
_____

Be still, and know that I am God.
—Psalm 46:10

3
_____

4

5

6

7

October

8

First keep yourself in peace, and then you will be able to pacify others. A peaceable man does more good than a learned one.
—Thomas à Kempis

9

10

11

12

13

14

October

15

16

17

18

19

*W*here there is
charity and wisdom,
there is neither fear nor
ignorance. Where there is
patience and humility,
there is neither anger nor
vexation. Where there is
poverty and joy, there is
neither greed nor avarice.
Where there is peace and
meditation, there is
neither anxiety nor doubt.
—St. Francis of Assisi

20

October

21

22

Resolved, to endeavor to my utmost to deny whatever is not most agreeable to a good, and universally sweet and benevolent, quiet, peaceable, contented, easy, compassionate, generous, humble, meek, modest, submissive, obliging, diligent and industrious, charitable, even, patient, moderate, forgiving, sincere temper; and to do at all times what such a temper would lead me to.
—Jonathan Edwards

23

24

25

October

26

I am an emptiness
for thee to fill; my soul a
cavern for thy sea.
—George MacDonald

27

28

October

29

30

Joy is like restless day; but peace divine like quiet night.
—Adelaide Anne Proctor

31

November

This most desirable Name is the soul of stillness and silence. By calling it to mind we gain joy and gladness, forgiveness of sins and a wealth of virtues. Few have been able to find this most glorious Name, save only in stillness and silence.
—Theophan the Recluse

November

1 _____

2 _____

3 _____

November

4

5

*Come to me, all who labour and are heavy
laden, and I will give you rest. Take my yoke upon
you, and learn from me; for I am gentle and lowly in
heart, and you will find rest for your souls. For my
yoke is easy, and my burden is light.*
—Jesus, quoted in Matthew 11:28-30

6

November

7

8

9

*To be glad of life
because it gives you the
chance to love and to
work and to play and to
look up at the stars;...
to covet nothing that is
your neighbor's except
his kindness of heart and
gentleness of manners—
to think seldom of your
enemies, often of your
friends, and every day
of Christ; and to spend
as much time as you
can, with body and with
spirit, in God's out-of-
doors—these are little
guideposts on the footpath
to peace.*
—Henry van Dyke

10

11

November

A peace above all earthly dignities,
A still and quiet conscience.
—William Shakespeare, *Henry VIII*

12

13

14

15

16

17

18

19

November

20

> *Father in heaven, when the thought of you wakes in our hearts, let it not awaken like a frightened bird flying about in dismay, but like a child waking from its sleep with a heavenly smile.*
> —Søren Kierkegaard

21

22

23

24

25

November

26

27

What the soul has to do in the time of quiet is only to be gentle and make no noise. ... Let the will quietly and prudently understand that one does not deal successfully with God by any efforts of one's own.
—St. Teresa of Avila

November

28

Any thought. . .upon which we lean will impede and disquiet us. It will make noise within the profound silence which we are given to possess for the sake of a deep and delicate listening. God speaks to the heart in this inner solitude.
—St. John of the Cross

29

30

December

*T*his is true peace, which stills and quiets the heart, not at the time when there is no misfortune but in the very midst of it, when outwardly nothing but discord meets the eye.
—Martin Luther

December

1

2

Peace and comfort can be found nowhere except in simple obedience.
—François Fénelon

3

December

4

5

6

7

December

8

9

10

Oh what blessedness it will be for a man, when he has reached his destination and rest, when he has become a being perfectly balanced, completely in harmony with himself and with the external conditions of his existence!
—Richard Rothe

December

11

12

13

December

14

O God, in the course of this busy life, give us times of refreshment and peace; and grant that we may so use our leisure to rebuild our bodies and renew our minds, that our spirits may be opened to the goodness of your creation.
—The Book of Common Prayer, 1977

15

16

17

18

19

20

December

21

22

Keep us, Lord, so awake in the duties of our calling that we may sleep in thy peace and wake in thy glory.
—John Donne

December

23

In silence man can most readily preserve his integrity.
—Meister Eckhert

24

25

December

26

27

28

December

29

30

There is no other way to life and to true inner peace than the way of the cross and of daily self-denial.
—Thomas à Kempis

31

Notes

Work is not always
required of a man. There
is such a thing as sacred
idleness, the cultivation
of which is now fearfully
neglected.
—George MacDonald

Notes

Notes

Notes

Notes

Notes

Notes

Notes

Painting Acknowledgements

January
Bowl with Flowers   Jan Van Der Sheer   Groningen, Netherlands

February
Studio Interior   Jan Van Loon   Groningen, Netherlands

March
Still Life with Pitcher and Shell   Edward Knippers   Arlington, W. Virginia USA

April
Shell   Henk Helmantel   Groningen, Netherlands

May
Still Life with Flowers   Jan Van Loon   Groningen, Netherlands

June
Violets   Jan Van Der Sheer   Groningen, Netherlands

Many thanks to J.P.L. Van Seventer of Art Revisited, Netherlands

Painting Acknowledgements

July
Watermelons and Tomatoes   Edward Kellogg   Sioux Center, Iowa USA

August
Still Life with Shell and Bottle   Jan Van Der Sheer   Groningen, Netherlands

September
Interior with Chair   Jan Van Loon   Groningen, Netherlands

October
Onions and Bean Pot   William Swetcharnik   Mount Airy, Maryland USA

November
Still Life with Sunflower   Jan Van Der Sheer   Groningen, Netherlands

December
Still Life with Blue Pot and Eggs   Henk Helmantel   Groningen, Netherlands

These paintings were assembled with the help of
Christians in the Arts Networking, Inc.   Cambridge, MA 02238-1941